Healthy Eating with MyPlate

Fruits

Nancy Dickmann

Heinemann Library
Chicago, Illinois

www.capstonepub.com
Visit our website to find out more information about Heinemann-Raintree books.

To order:
Phone 800-747-4992
Visit www.capstonepub.com
to browse our catalog and order online.

Edited by Rebecca Rissman and Adrian Vigliano
Designed by Joanna Hinton-Malivoire
Picture research by Elizabeth Alexander
Production by Victoria Fitzgerald
Originated by Capstone Global Library Ltd

Library of Congress Cataloging-in-Publication Data
Cataloging-in-Publication data is on file at the Library of Congress.

ISBN 978-1-4329-6973-8 (hc) -- ISBN 978-1-4329-6980-6 (pb)

Acknowledgements
We would like to thank the following for permission to reproduce photographs: Alamy: age fotostock, 10, Bloom Works Inc., 11, PureStock, 15; Capstone Studio: Karon Dubke, Cover, 22; Getty Images: Alistair Berg, 17, hphimagelibrary, 20, 23 middle, John Smith, 9, 23 bottom, Radius Images, 16, Rosemary Calvert, 8; iStockphoto: Elena Korenbaum, 7, Mark Hatfield, 23 top, viafilms, 5; Shutterstock: arek_malang, Back Cover, 13, Denis and Yulia Pogostins, 4, Dreams Come True, 21, Georgios Alexandris, 6, Monkey Business Images, 18, Simone van den Berg, 12, VCoscaron, 14; U.S. Department of Agriculture, Center for Nutrition Policy and Promotion, 19

Every effort has been made to contact copyright holders of material reproduced in this book. Any omissions will be rectified in subsequent printings if notice is given to the publishers.

Printed in the United States 5619

Contents

What Are Fruits?

Fruits are parts of plants.

Eating fruits can keep us healthy.

Some fruits grow on trees.

Some fruits grow on vines.

Looking at Fruits

Many fruits are round.

Fruits can be many different colors.

We dry some fruits. Raisins are dried grapes.

We make juice from some fruits.

How Fruits Help Us

Fruits are full of nutrients.

You need nutrients to stay healthy.

Eating bananas keeps your blood healthy.

Eating kiwis helps you fight colds.

Eating fruits helps your body make energy.

You need energy to work
and play.

Healthy Eating

Half of the foods you eat each day should be fruits or vegetables.

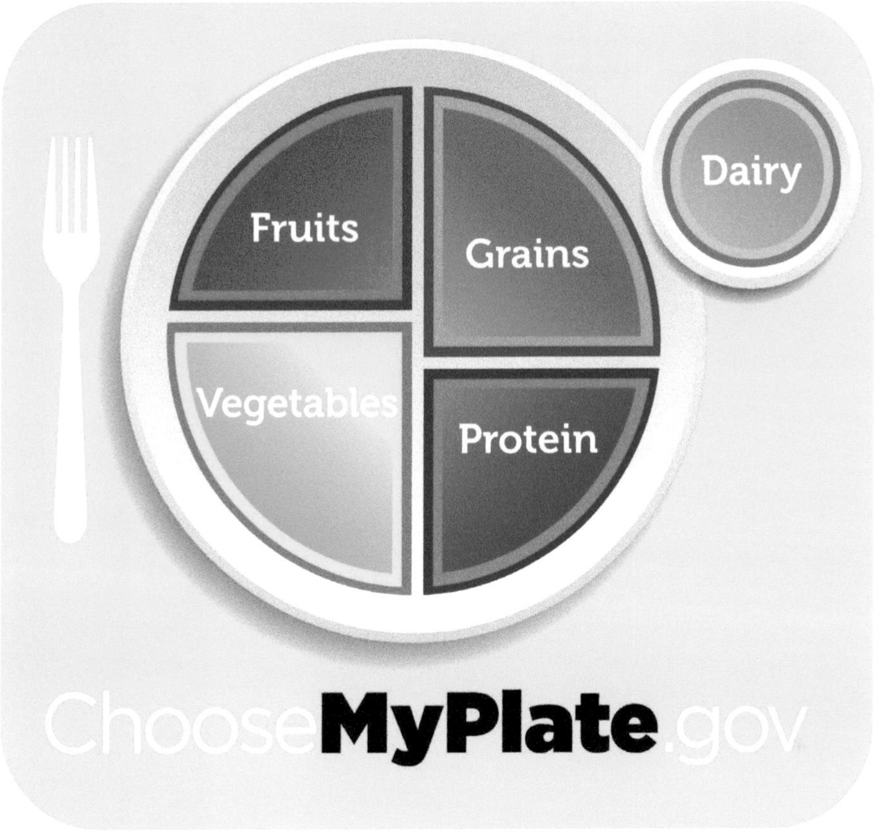

MyPlate reminds us to eat some foods from each food group every day.

Staying Healthy

We eat fruits to stay healthy.

We eat fruits because they taste good!

Find the Fruits

Here is a healthy breakfast.

Can you find the fruits?

Answer on page 24

Picture Glossary

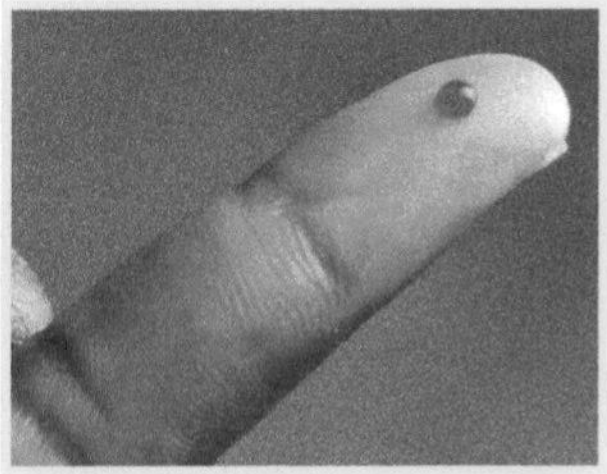

blood red liquid inside your body. Blood takes food and air to all your body parts.

energy the power to do something. We need energy when we work or play.

nutrients things our bodies need to stay healthy. You can get nutrients in different foods.

Index

Answer to quiz on page 22: The fruits include the strawberries in the bowl, and the oranges that have been made into orange juice in the glass.

Notes to parents and teachers

Before reading

Explain that we need to eat a range of different foods to stay healthy. Splitting foods into different groups can help us understand how much food we should eat from each group. Introduce the fruits element on the MyPlate graphic on page 19. Draw children's attention to the fact that half of MyPlate is made up of fruits and vegetables. This means half of what they eat should be fruits and vegetables. Encourage children to eat a variety of fruits every day.

After reading

- Play "Guess the mystery fruit." Place a fruit or fruit picture into a bag. Alternatively, choose a fruit from the cover of this book. Give the children clues to help them identify the fruit. For example, "It has seeds. It tastes sour. It grows on a tree." Take turns describing different fruits.
- Ask children to bring in some fruits. These could be their favorite fruits or fruits they have never tried before. Share the fruits with the class. Explain that our taste buds change and why it is good to try new things. Create a pictogram to show the class's favorite fruits.
- Ask children to sit in a circle with one child standing in the center. Choose four different fruits and give one fruit name to each child. When the child in the center calls out a fruit, everyone with that fruit name should swap places. The child in the center should try to find a place to sit. The caller can also choose to call out "fruit salad." If they do so, everyone in the circle needs to swap places.